Howie's Hungabird Dilemma

Sandy Baker

Illustrated by Casie Trace

Black Garnet Press
Santa Rosa, CA

Howie's Hungabird Dilemma

Black Garnet Press
P.O. Box 2914
Santa Rosa, CA 95405

To Bud, a Humdinger of a Husband

Text Copyright © 2014 by Sandy Baker
Illustrations Copyright © 2014 by Casie Trace

ISBN 978-0-9832383-9-3

Designed by Rita Ter Sarkissoff • www.springhillbooks.com • Printed in USA

Also by Sandy Baker

Color My Garden (English and Spanish versions) 2013
The Dead Butterflies Diary, 2013
Zack's Zany Zucchiniland, 2012
Mrs. Feeny and the Grubby Garden Gang, 2011
The Tehran Triangle (with Tom Reed), 2012

Visit the author's website for more information at www.sandybakerwriter.com

Whooossh! Swooossh! *Schwissh!*

"Oh no, Mrs. Hatcher is at it again," said Howie. "Hungabirds!" shouted three-year old Carole Ann.

Why in the world does she try to hurt the tiniest of all birds, Howie wondered. *I gotta figure out how to stop her.*

Zzzzip, whizzzz!

🌸 3

Howie dragged Carole Ann into the house to tell their mom.
"Mrs. Hatcher's crazy! Look at her—trying to whack the hummingbirds with her tennis racquet! They just want food—they're not safe over there."

"Howie, maybe she has a reason," said his mother.

"Mo-om, nobody hates hummingbirds. It seems like they're teasing her. She hasn't hit one yet, but I'm afraid it's gonna happen. Look, their acrobatics are cool, aren't they?"

"Wanna see," begged Carole Ann. "Wanna see hungabirds."
"Up we go," said Howie. "See how she's chasing them."

Howie learned at school that they can't walk. "See, Carole Ann, they fly forwards and backwards and hover, but not walk 'cause their little feet are curled, for hanging onto tiny branches."

"The feeder outside our kitchen window is the best!" Howie said. "Seems like the hummers are always looking for food. They catch tiny insects, too. Wonder if they get tired flying around all day?"

"Let's make a fresh batch of sugar-water, Howie," offered his mom. They carefully measured four cups of water, one cup of sugar. Howie boiled the water and then helped Carole Ann while they added the sugar and stirred it real well. He rinsed the feeder with hot water before refilling it.

🌸 9

"I heard that food coloring isn't healthy for hummingbirds," he said.

"Most feeders are red anyway," Mom said, "Just to attract the hummers. How do you know that?"

"My teacher told me," said Howie. "Wow, look at their feathers,
Carole Ann—green, red, pink, brownish, and that one is sparkly shiny."

"See how that brownish one is trying to keep the others away from the feeder?" Mom pointed out. "Some hummingbirds are bullies, Carole Ann. But the other ones just ignore them, fly away, and come back. No fights!"

"Bully hungabirds," repeated Carole Ann.

"Yeah, do you know what else, Mom? Hummingbirds like flowers with dangly little bells or trumpets. Their long bill can reach right in. And red is definitely their favorite color."

"Right," said Mom. "See how the hummers seem to go for the red ones, Carole Ann?"

"You know what's so fun? If I hold the hose very still, the hummers fly through it, sip water and fluff their feathers," he said. "They can't even bathe in a birdbath like other birds because their feet can't walk."

Howie peeked out the window. *Oh, not again. Mrs. Hatcher is up to her old tricks, trying to bat away the hummingbirds.*

"I gotta go, Mom. I can't let Mrs. Hatcher hurt them. You know, I think I figured it out!" Howie left the house with Carole Ann trailing behind.

Before he even noticed, Carole Ann bolted over to Mrs. Hatcher and screamed "Lemme, lemme." She hung on tight while Mrs. Hatcher looked like an angry Halloween mask and tried to shake her off.

"Oh, sheesh, Carole Ann," said Howie.

"Well, really, Howie," Mrs. Hatcher huffed. "This is the last thing I expected from this three-year old."

"Sor-ry," he said. "We just don't like the way you swing at the hummers is all. They like being around you and I'm pretty sure I know why."

"No, Howie, they do not like me, and I definitely don't like them," she said, swinging her racquet again.

"But, Mrs. Hatcher . . . "

"Don' hurt hungabirds, Mizatcher," cried Carole Ann.

🌸 19

"They want to poke out my eye with their long, pointy bills."
"No, wait . . ." said Howie.
"I'll show them!" she said.

Schwissh! *Whooosh!*

❀ 20

"No, please," Howie begged. "They're checking out your red sun hat to see if it's a flower—red is their favorite color. That's all. When I wear a red T-shirt, they hang around me, too. Just wear a different color hat. You'll see."

Howie kept a lookout next door. Later that afternoon, he saw Mrs. Hatcher tiptoeing into her garden wearing a straw sun hat. She ducked like she was expecting low-flying hummingbirds.

"Come on, Carole Ann. Let's go see Mrs. Hatcher again" said Howie. "Hi, Mrs. Hatcher, sorry about before."

"Howie, the hummingbirds are going for my snapdragons and red coral bells," she said, laughing as she watched the hummers sip nectar at each bloom.

Whirrr, zooommm, zzzip.

"See, I told ya, Mrs. Hatcher, no red hat, no dive-bombing hummers!" he said. "Look, they love red. Did ya know that they pollinate flowers?"

"Hmmm, almost like bees," Mrs. Hatcher agreed.

"Hungabirds pretty."

"In a couple of months, most will fly south where it's warmer. Then after the winter, they'll come right back here to *your* garden," said Howie. "They have built-in radar or something. Betcha!"

🌸 25

"Are you sure, Howie? I hope they return. Come here, Carole Ann, let's watch the hummingbirds."

"Love hungabirds!"

"No more tennis racquet, Mrs. Hatcher?"

"No tennis racquet, I promise, kids."

Glossary

Aerobatics .... Like acrobatics in the air; flying feats of rolls, dives, and climbs.

Brood .... A family of young birds or other animals.

Bully .... An animal or person that picks on a weaker one; can be abusive or cruel.

Camouflage .... A disguise, something that makes a thing look like something else.

Display dive ...... During courting season, male hummingbirds soar to more than 100 feet in the air and then dive downward, their tail feathers creating a strange explosion of noise. The guys are "showing off" for the girls!

Fatal .... Deadly, causing death.

Hazard .... Something that's risky or dangerous.

Iridescent .... A shiny, show of brilliant colors from the effect of light.

Maneuver .... A very clever movement involving changes of direction, position, speed.

Nectar .... A sweet liquid in a flower; bees, hummingbirds, and butterflies need it to survive and search for it during the day.

Nourishment ..... Food and drinks that sustain life and promote good health.

Pollinator .... Insect or animal that carries pollen from one part of the flower to another, fertilizing the flower to make seeds.

Predators .... An enemy that tracks, kills, and eats another.

Preen .... Birds preen by removing dirt and parasites from their feathers, straightening out their feathers for better flying and waterproofing, and to look sleek for attracting a mate.

Roost .... To settle down and sleep overnight on a perch, protected branch, or even a roof or beam.

Rouse .... To wake up and come out of a sleepy or inactive state.

Tubular .... Trumpet- or bell-like in shape; long, narrow and hollow, as in some flower blooms.

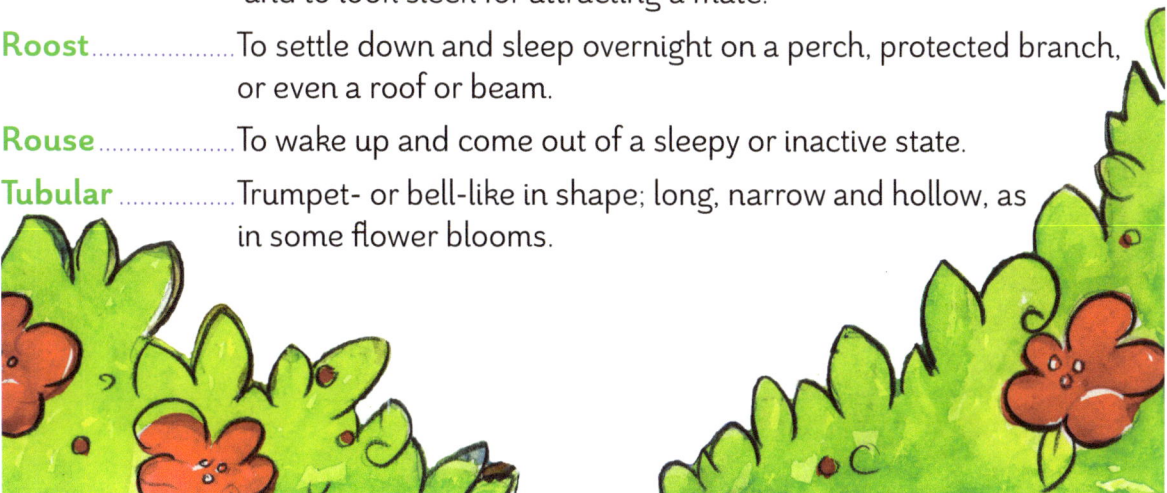

Fun Facts About Hummingbirds

🌸 **The smallest** hummingbird is about 2 ¼ inches long while the more common Anna's is an inch larger. It's about as heavy as a penny!

🌸 **The hummingbird** bill is long and tubular, sometimes straight, sometimes curved. Its length and shape help get nectar from deep, narrow flowers. The bird's split tongue drains the nectar from the flower.

🌸 **Hummingbirds are** found only in the Americas. There are about 340 species with only 17 that breed in the United States. Four or five other species are "visitors."

🌸 **Do hummingbirds** sing? They do, but they sing so fast that our ears hear only chirps, squeaks, and twits. The other sound we hear is the humming of their wings beating rapidly. That's how they got their common name of hummingbirds!

🌸 **The normal** speed of a hummingbird is about 25-30 miles per hour. Its wings can stroke 80 beats per second, and as many as 200 beats in a display dive. Sometimes hummingbirds can fly up to 65 miles per hour.

🌸 **Hummingbirds are** famous for their fancy aerobatics. They can fly forward, backward, hover, roll, dive, and maneuver just about any which way.

🌸 **Because hummingbirds** fly at very fast speeds and use a lot of energy, they must feed every ten minutes or so during the day. They thrive on nectar plus tiny insects and spiders for protein.

🌸 **Many of** the hummingbird's feathers are iridescent, especially those on the head, throat, and neck. The brilliant, shiny colors appear because light reflected on the feathers causes the colors to change depending upon the angle of that light.

- Hummingbirds have a few predators, like hawks, crows and other larger birds, but one of the biggest hazards for them is clear window glass. The reflections of trees, shrubs, and clouds on the glass attract them. Flying into the glass is often fatal.

- Sometimes weather can be dangerous to hummingbirds. In long spells of cold or rain or hot, dry weather, the flowers that the birds need for survival won't grow and bloom to feed them.

- Courting, mating, and nesting season can begin as early as December for some.

- The female builds the tiny nest, often about 1½ inches across. It's shaped like a cup and lined with plant down or sometimes the fluff from clothes dryers. The outside is camouflaged with lichen and moss, held together with spider webs.

- The pure white hummingbird eggs are only about ½ inch long. Once a year, most moms lay two or sometimes three eggs. However, the Allen's and Rufous have two broods per year, and the Anna's and Black-chinned as many as three.

- When the weather turns cold, most hummingbirds fly thousands of miles to their warm over-wintering homes in Mexico and Central America. Some species, like the Anna's, are year-round inhabitants in warmer climates.

- Do hummingbirds sleep? Yes, they roost overnight in dense foliage. Their heart rate slows down so that the little birds can appear dead. They are not. At dawn, they rouse and begin looking for nourishment.

- Do hummingbirds need water? Definitely. They sip droplets of heavy dew, water collected in leaves, or from a garden fountain, birdbath, or sprinkler. They often bathe on the fly or dip down into shallow birdbaths and then preen their feathers while perching on a nearby branch or wire.

- Hummingbirds have no sense of smell. They must find their food by seeing it. That's why bright red flowers attract them.

Some Favorite Hummingbird Flowers

- ✳ Agave
- ✳ Bee Balm
- ✳ Bouvardia
- ✳ California Fuchsia
- ✳ Cape Honeysuckle
- ✳ Cardinal Flower
- ✳ Columbine
- ✳ Coral Bells
- ✳ Delphinium
- ✳ Flowering Currant
- ✳ Flowering Maple
- ✳ Flowering Quince
- ✳ Four-o-clocks
- ✳ Gladiola
- ✳ Hibiscus
- ✳ Hollyhocks
- ✳ Impatiens
- ✳ Indian Paintbrush
- ✳ Lantana
- ✳ Larkspur
- ✳ Lupine
- ✳ Mexican Bush Sage
- ✳ Mexican Sunflower
- ✳ Penstemon
- ✳ Petunia
- ✳ Phlox
- ✳ Pineapple Sage
- ✳ Nasturtium
- ✳ Red Hot Poker
- ✳ Rose Mallow
- ✳ Scarlet Monkey Flower
- ✳ Scarlet Sage
- ✳ Spider Flower
- ✳ Texas Sage
- ✳ Trumpet Creeper
- ✳ Trumpet Honeysuckle

References and Reading

Charles, Susan G., *Hummingbirds: All About Hummingbirds, A Kids Introduction to Hummers—Fun Facts & Pictures About the Worlds Smallest Bird* (Sep 14, 2013)

Stokes, Donald and Stokes, Lillian, *The Hummingbird Book: The Complete Guide to Attracting, Identifying, and Enjoying Hummingbirds* (Nov 16, 2008)

Strattin, Lisa , *Facts About Hummingbirds: Hummingbirds Picture Book for Kids (Facts for Kids Picture Books)* (Nov 30, 2013)

Tilford, Tony, *The Complete Book of Hummingbirds* (Mar 1, 2009)

http://nationalzoo.si.edu/scbi/migratorybirds/webcam/hummingbirds.cfm

http://www.hummingbirdsociety.org/index.php

http://www.worldofhummingbirds.com/facts.php

http://birds.audubon.org/hummingbirds-home

About the Author

Two years ago, when Sandy Baker moved from the country into town, she left behind seventy hummingbirds. The new home and garden came with none, that is, until she planted salvia, rosemary, hollyhocks, and hung up a feeder. Now, four hummers grace Sandy's garden. Other than admiring hummingbirds, Sandy writes and gardens. Her garden is jammed with as many flowers as possible to attract birds, bees, butterflies, and bugs. Sandy enjoys traveling with her husband. She takes scads of photographs, especially of beautiful gardens. You can see plenty more about gardening, hummingbirds, and butterflies on Sandy's kid-friendly website www.sandybakerwriter.com.

About the Illustrator

Casie Pace Trace grew up with pens and paintbrushes in her hand in Macon GA where she still lives. Her parents always encouraged her passion in art. Casie graduated from Georgia College & State University with a BA in Studio Art, concentrating in Painting. Her dream of illustrating a children's book came true with Howie. Her other dreams include traveling to faraway places and eventually owning a board game coffee shop and bakery with her husband. Casie encourages all children to follow their passions! You can view more of her work at casietrace.com.

Acknowledgements

Once again, I am grateful to Rita Ter Sarkissoff for her superb work on *Howie's Hungabird Dilemma*, the fourth book she has designed for me. She combines her extensive knowledge of the publication process with her excellent design skills, always presenting fresh ideas. We continue to work via email—perhaps one of these years we'll meet. Illustrator Casie Trace and I discovered each other through the blogosphere. What a serendipitous meeting! She perfectly captures Howie and little Carole Ann with her colorful and charming illustrations. And of course I am happy to be a Sonoma County Master Gardener, now in my 14th year. MGs are the best source of support, encouragement, and friendship—plus all that useful gardening information!

www.ingramcontent.com/pod-product-compliance
Lightning Source LLC
Chambersburg PA
CBHW041553040426
42447CB00002B/162